SEARCH FOR THE BLACK RHINO

BY ALISON GILLIGAN

ILLUSTRATED BY VLADIMIR SEMIONOV
COVER ILLUSTRAT~~ED~~ ~~by~~ BHOR UTOMO

CH~~OOSE~~

WAITSF~~IELD~~

D0354729

BEWARE and WARNING!

This book is different from other books.

You and YOU ALONE are in charge of what happens in this story.

There are dangers, choices, adventures, and consequences. YOU must use all of your numerous talents and much of your enormous intelligence. The wrong decision could end in disaster—even death. But, don't despair. At any time, YOU can go back and make another choice, alter the path of your story, and change its result.

YOU join your parents on a modern day safari to Lake Nakuru, Kenya, hoping to see one of the rarest animals on earth. Your days will be filled with exotic sights, sounds, tastes, and customs...not to mention man-eating lions, nasty tsetse flies, and the occasional flash flood.

Kids love reading
Choose Your Own Adventure®!

"These books are like games. Sometimes the choice seems like it will solve everything, but you wonder if it's a trap."

Matt Harmon, age 11

"I think you'd call this a book for active readers, and I am definitely an active reader!"

Ava Kendrick, age 11

"You decide your own fate, but your fate is still a surprise."

Chun Tao Lin, age 10

"Come on in this book if you're crazy enough! One wrong move and you're a goner!"

Ben Curley, age 9

"You can read *Choose Your Own Adventure* books so many wonderful ways. You could go find your dog or follow a unicorn."

Celia Lawton, age 11

*This book is dedicated to
Diana and Terry*

Illustrated by: Vladimir Semionov
Cover Art: Gabhor Utomo
Cover and Book Design: Julia Gignoux,
Freedom Hill Design and Book Production

For information regarding permission, write to:

CHOOSECO®
P.O. Box 46
Waitsfield, Vermont 05673
www.cyoa.com

ISBN-13: 978-1-937133-01-6
ISBN-10: 1-937133-01-X

Published simultaneously in the United States and Canada

Printed in the Canada

0 9 8 7 6 5 4 3 2 1

BRRRIIINNNGGG!!!

The final bell! It's your last day of school before the start of your two-week Spring Break. You're about to head off on a safari to Kenya with your parents.

You've been looking forward to this trip for a long time. Your mother is the Senior Vertebrate Zoologist at the American Museum of Natural History in New York City, where you live. She specializes in *perissodactyls*—better known as hoofed animals like horses. Her particular specialty is the rare black rhino. One of the reasons you're going on safari is so that she can observe and research black rhinos in the wild.

Your father was born in London but immigrated to the United States more than twenty years ago. He is co-head of a family-owned company, Jamoke. Jamoke imports coffee from the family's plantation on the Laikipia Plateau near Mt. Kenya. Bennett—his brother, partner, and your favorite uncle—lives in Kenya and runs the plantation.

Recently you heard your dad and Uncle Bennett on a video call. They were talking about the declining price for Jamoke coffee at Nairobi's coffee auctions. They're both puzzled about why it's happening.

Turn to the next page.

2

You hurry home to finish packing. When you unlock the door to your brownstone apartment, you immediately spot a stranger's hat and wooden cane on the hall table. The cane resembles an elaborately carved reptile. You hear voices so you quietly shut the front door and edge nearer the living room to listen.

"Remember Elizabeth," says a deep, resonant voice to your mother. "Keep a close eye on LJ during the safari. It's vital that we pass along as much information to the FBI as soon as possible."

"I will," your mother says, her voice rising, "But I don't deny that I'm scared. These people are serious criminals dealing in serious money. This is a little outside my normal job description."

FBI, criminals, money?! you think to yourself. *What's this all about?*

You cough loudly to announce your arrival. Your mother looks startled at first but quickly recovers. "I'd like you to meet Dr. James Abellera, the museum's Chief Zoologist. And one of the world's greatest scientists," she says to you.

"Your mother exaggerates," Dr. Abellera says, with a twinkle in his eye. He shakes your hand. His grip is very strong.

Turn to page 4.

"Have a wonderful time in Africa," he continues. "The most fascinating—and perhaps dangerous—place on Earth."

As soon as he leaves, your mother reminds you to finish packing. You'll have to probe her about the mysterious LJ later tonight.

That evening you and your parents sit down for a delicious dinner of take-out sushi from Kyoko's, your favorite neighborhood restaurant. You and your dad tease your mom because she always orders the same "safe" dish—chicken teriyaki and rice. It's certainly tasty, but you and your dad are more adventurous eaters and often challenge each other to try the most exotic thing on the menu. You're proudly convinced it's a genetic trait you both share. Tonight the most exotic offering is tricolored fish roe wrapped in a seaweed cone. You and your dad have placed double orders for it.

"This is amazing!" you say, your mouth full of food.

Your mother winces and crinkles her nose. You're not sure if it's from the idea of three different colored fish eggs, you talking with a full mouth of food, or maybe she's worried about "LJ" and your upcoming safari.

Go on to the next page.

You and your dad chatter throughout the dinner about all the things you're looking forward to in Kenya—the safari, the animals, the sights and sounds of Africa, and a chance to visit with Uncle Bennett.

"Do you think he'll remember the family song?" you ask, hopefully.

Your dad laughs. "Java Jive! It's not really a family song," he tells you. "Just one of my favorite tunes. I used to sing it to you when you were a baby instead of nursery rhymes. And of course Bennett will remember it—do you?"

Together you begin singing.

Your mom smiles at the two of you but doesn't join in. You can tell she's distracted and more than a little worried about today's events.

Turn to the next page.

6

In the rush of dinner, organizing, and packing you never get the chance to ask your mother about what you overheard this afternoon. Later while lying in bed, you hear your parents whispering in the hallway near your bedroom door. Their voices are low but you clearly hear your father tell your mother, "Whatever you do, please be careful. These people are dangerous. They must never feel threatened or else..." his voice drifts away as you begin to fall asleep.

Even though you are tired, you spend a restless night, tossing and turning. Your dreams are full of dark shadows, strange sounds, and creepy visions. Finally, near dawn, you fall into deep, dreamless sleep.

Go on to the next page.

BEEP!BEEP! BEEP!BEEP!

Your alarm clock wakes you up a few hours later. You stumble through a shower, throw on some clothes, grab your bags, and meet your parents at the front door. Two very long plane rides later you walk out of Jomo Kenyatta International Airport and into the hot, humid, chaotic, and amazing city of Nairobi.

You and your parents grab a taxi to the Ambassador Hotel, a former colonial outpost built during the 1920s when Britain ruled the country. Although Kenya gained its independence in 1963, some British influences still remain—including a love of coffee and tea.

You take a nap to help recover from jet lag. You're very reluctant to get out of your soft, warm bed until your mother whispers in your ear, "Uncle Bennett is downstairs and he can't wait to see you!"

Your uncle is both fun and funny, full of exotic tales about life in Kenya on the coffee plantation. You scramble out of bed, throw on a clean shirt, and race downstairs.

You spot your father and uncle in the lobby café, sharing a pot of coffee. They're deep in conversation. You decide to surprise your uncle and sneak up behind him.

Turn to the next page.

As you get closer, you hear Uncle Bennett tell your father, "It makes no sense. We're producing some of the finest coffee on the plateau, but our recent auction prices are way too low. I think someone is trying to sabotage us!"

Your arrival stops the conversation cold. Uncle Bennett greets you warmly, but you can tell he's worried. He glances at your father, and then again at you.

"I have a special request," he says to you, cautiously. "Your father's already given his approval."

You can tell this is serious. You swallow hard.

"I know you're a bit of a math wizard," he continues. He pulls a thick stack of papers from his leather satchel.

"These are all the auction results for Kenya's largest coffee producers for the past year, including us. These contain all sorts of info—bean gradings, high and low prices, and amounts sold. I need you to make some sense of this mess and help us find out why Jamoke's recent prices are so low."

You readily agree. You'll do anything to help your family.

Although you spend the evening together touring lively Nairobi, a cloud seems to hang over your uncle and dad. The twinkle in Uncle Bennett's eye is gone and your father looks troubled. You try to cheer them up by humming "Java Jive," but neither one joins in. Even a dinner of the favorite local dish, porridge-like ugali and fish, doesn't seem to make them happy. Something's not right and you're determined to investigate this "coffee sabotage" further.

Turn to the next page.

10

The next morning you all gather together in the hotel café for breakfast. The plan is for your parents to meet their safari guide and then head off to Lake Nakuru. You'll accompany Uncle Bennett back to the family's plantation for a few days and then meet up with your parents on safari toward the end of the week.

Suddenly, an Asian man dressed in khaki pants, a white linen shirt, and a bushmaster safari hat walks up to your table. His eyes dart among you nervously.

"Habari, bibi," he says in Swahili, offering his hand to your mother. He quickly switches to English. "Mrs. Elizabeth—I'm very happy to meet you and your family. I recognized you from the photo Dr. Abellera sent me. My name is Lee Jong, and I'm your chief safari guide."

Lee Jong, you think quickly. LJ! Could this be the criminal you heard Dr. Abellera mention to your mother? If you leave with Uncle Bennett, will your parents be safe on safari with him?

If you choose to go with Uncle Bennett to the family's coffee plantation to investigate the coffee sabotage, turn to page 12.

If you choose to go with your parents and the mysterious Lee Jong on safari, turn to page 42.

You decide to stay with the plan and leave with Uncle Bennett. You head north out of Nairobi, riding together in his open-air jeep. The crowded, chaotic landscape of the city is soon replaced by a beautifully calm and expansive countryside, shining in the African sun.

The landscape changes again to cool, dense woodlands as you climb in altitude. The family's plantation, Jamoke Coffee, is on the Laikipia Plateau in the shadow of Mt. Kenya. That majestic peak rises more than 12,500 feet above sea level and is a favorite climb for serious mountaineers.

Your uncle drives through the plantation's front gate. You continue down the long dirt and gravel driveway toward the big house.

You feel a deep connection to this land. Your great-grandparents started this plantation in 1924, and it's been run by your family ever since.

On either side of the drive are long, well-groomed rows of *Coffea arabica* plants, a tree-like bush with glossy green leaves that produces the prized coffee that the Jamoke brand is famous for. All the bushes are dotted with beautiful white flowers.

"They're in bloom!" you cry excitedly. Uncle Bennett gleams at you.

Go on to the next page.

"The blossoms are very big this year," he says with pride. "Once those flowers turn into coffee berries, we should have a record crop."

The plantation foreman, Mosi, greets you with a bear hug. Mosi's family has been working on the plantation since your great-grandparents' day. He is a jovial and hard-working man, and you've heard your father say many times that they could never produce such good coffee without him.

Over the years your father and uncle have deeded parcels of land to Mosi and his three daughters, knowing that one day he will leave to start his own coffee company with his family. Until then he continues to work for your family and collect the profits that his share of the land produces.

Turn to page 15.

"Wewe mzima kubwa kama ng'ombe!" he says to you. [You have grown as big as an ox!]

"Si ng'ombe lakini labda ni mbwa kubwa!" you reply. [Not an ox but maybe a big dog!] Suddenly you're very glad your father has made you take all those Swahili lessons. You'll need the language if you're going to work on the plantation one day.

Reluctantly Mosi turns toward your uncle. "Gitonga," he says in English, calling your uncle by his local nickname, which means "wealthy one." "We have two problems that need quick attention." He pauses before continuing, glancing toward you.

"It's all right," Uncle Bennett says gently. "If he's going to be involved in the business one day, he may as well start learning about it now."

"Our coffee again sold for a low price at this week's auction," Mosi says with disappointment.

"And problem number two?" you uncle asks, frowning.

"It's the bushes at the far southwest corner of the land," Mosi replies. "Something—or some-one—trampled a whole bunch of them last night. Nearly a dozen bushes have been destroyed. We need to figure out what's going on there before we lose any more of our crop."

If you decide to help investigate the coffee auction problem first, turn to the next page.

If you decide to inspect the trampled coffee crops, turn to page 31.

16

"I think I'll take a look at those sales reports," you tell your Uncle, patting the satchel at your side.

"Good idea," he replies before heading off with Mosi.

You pore over all of the documents your uncle gave you, examining coffee prices at the weekly Nairobi Coffee Exchange auctions. You quickly learn that coffee is rated based on the size of the beans after they've been milled. AA grade beans receive the highest prices at auction; T grade receive the lowest. The coffee is packed in sisal bags that hold 60 kilos each. Every coffee house packs its own bags for auction.

According to the sales receipts, until recently the Jamoke brand had consistently sold at the top of the price range for about $400 per bag of beans. However, starting about two months ago the average price dropped to about $360 per bag.

You develop an elaborate spreadsheet, tracking all the information you've been given—the dates, the grades of the coffee, the auction prices, and the amounts sold for all the top producers.

"The coffee we're selling is the same quality, month to month," you later tell your uncle gravely, laying out the pages of your spreadsheet before him. "But just like you suspected, all the other plantations are getting good prices for their AA beans while only our prices have dropped. It doesn't happen all the time but often enough to make me suspicious."

Go on to the next page.

You continue cautiously, "I have a vague idea what's wrong but I want to confirm something first. I need to secretly go to the coffee auction this Tuesday. It's important you don't tell anyone I'm there. "

Your uncle looks very concerned but finally agrees with you.

That night you rework a formula based on which employee is bringing the coffee to auction. Mosi and your uncle have said they don't suspect any of the Jamoke employees. You worry that maybe they're a little too trusting.

Eureka! You're positive you've found the answer. Every time Mosi's oldest daughter takes the beans to auction, the Jamoke brand gets a good price. But every time Mjanja, a relatively new employee, brings the crop to auction, the price declines.

Coincidentally, Mjanja started a little over three months ago. He came with the recommendation of a fellow coffee grower from the Kisii plantation. The plantation had fallen on hard times and had to lay off many of the employees. Mjanja was fortunate to find a new job so quickly.

Your luck continues. Checking the schedule you see that Mjanja is due to bring the coffee to auction this week.

Later that night you drift off to sleep, a big smile on your face as you imagine an "A+" at the top of your spreadsheet—the mark you hope Mr. Bailey will give you for this project when you return to school.

Turn to the next page.

18

Very early Tuesday morning you climb into the back of the Jamoke truck hauling the coffee to auction. You wedge yourself between full sacks of beans and wait. Soon the engine roars to life and you suffer through a long, bumpy ride to Nairobi.

Once the truck stops, you quickly hop out, not wanting to be seen. You hide behind some wooden crates and watch as Mjanja and another worker climb out of the truck. Mjanja tells the worker he's free to head into town to see his family.

"What?" the young worker asks, surprised. "I'm here to help you unload the coffee. I'm supposed to keep an eye on it until it's our turn at auction."

The worker continues cautiously. "Mosi is my boss. I don't think he'd approve of me neglecting my work."

"Don't worry about it," Mjanja says smoothly. "Mosi is a taskmaster. Everyone knows that."

Mjanja smiles broadly. "You work so hard for the company. Take a little time off. Go see your family, enjoy yourself."

Go on to the next page.

A little reluctantly the worker heads out the warehouse door. Just then a tall, chubby man approaches Mjanja. He has a huge scar on his face, all the way from his left ear to the corner of his nose.

He and Mjanja talk together quietly. The man with the scar signals to a nearby forklift operator. A pallet of Kisii brand coffee rolls into view. You know that brand from your spreadsheet! They produce an inferior crop of beans, nothing higher than B grade.

You watch in horror as Mjanja pulls out a stack of Jamoke labels and begins attaching them to all the Kisii bags on the pallet. When he's done, the man with the scar hands over a stack of Kisii labels. Together they pull bags of Jamoke coffee off the truck, cover up the Jamoke name on each sisal bag with a Kisii label, and then load them onto the forklift.

Turn to the next page.

When they've finished switching all the labels, the man with the scar hands Mjanja a thick envelope. Mjanja looks inside, smiles widely, shakes his hand, and walks toward the door. The man with the scar directs the forklift holding the fake Jamoke coffee through the auction room door.

You run to the exit just in time to see Mjanja reach the end of the parking lot. He is escaping! You could run after him but you're not sure what direction he's going.

You know that Mosi is in town on business today. You could go find him and tell him what you've seen.

Just then you hear the auctioneer announce in a booming voice, "Next up—lot number 249, forty-five bags of Premium Grade AA coffee from the Jamoke Company."

If you choose to follow Mjanja, turn to page 22.

If you choose to follow the man with the scar into the auction, turn to page 25.

If you choose to go find Mosi, turn to page 29.

There's no time to lose! You follow Mjanja down the street, careful to stay at least half a block behind him. You watch as he enters the Kenyan National Bank.

Through the large plate glass window you watch Mjanja take the fat envelope out of his pocket and silently count the money inside. He fills out a deposit slip and approaches a teller. While his back is turned, you quietly sneak into the bank and hide behind a potted fichus tree.

The teller hands Mjanja a receipt. He smiles at her warmly. "One last request," he says to her. "I'd like a printout of all my account activity, including recent deposits and my current balance."

Mjanja takes the paper and walks toward the window, reading it in the bright sunlight. You're only a few feet away. Your heart is racing in fear of being caught. However, Mjanja is completely absorbed in his task.

He smiles in satisfaction, crumples up the paper, and tosses it into a nearby trash can. He heads out the door. You quickly follow Mjanja but first retrieve the crumpled paper from the trash, stuffing it into your pocket.

Go on to the next page.

Mjanja crosses the street and enters the Nairobi Holiday Travel Agency. The office is small and empty except for a woman behind a desk. If you followed him in, there's no doubt he'd see you. You're forced to watch from outside, crouched near the door.

He has an animated conversation with the woman. She quickly types something on her computer keyboard and turns the screen so Mjanja can see the results. It looks like a long list of flights.

Mjanja glances at his watch and points to something in the middle of the screen. The travel agent smiles broadly, does a little more computer work, and hands Mjanja a printed ticket. He pays in cash and approaches the entrance.

You jump up and hide between two parked cars. Mjanja hails a taxi, hops in, and zooms away. You run to the street to grab the next available cab. You plead with the driver to go as fast as he can to catch up to Mjanja's taxi.

Soon you're back at the Jomo Kenyatta International Airport. You watch in dismay as Mjanja approaches the Air France counter. He trades in his ticket for a boarding pass on the next flight to Paris and heads toward the gate.

You can only follow him to the end of the security line. Without a ticket the stern security guard won't let you go any farther.

Turn to the next page.

24

You see Mjanja stroll toward his gate. You watch him until he is out of sight. In frustration you stuff your hands into your pockets—and happily discover the forgotten bank report.

Mjanja may be trying to escape, but you have all his bank account information. Surely your uncle and Mosi can use this to convince the police to arrest him when he lands in Paris—can't they?

The End

You follow the man with the scar into the coffee auction. As the forklift clears the door, an inspector cuts a small hole in the top of several bags of coffee, removes a few beans from each, and examines them under a digital fluorescence microscope. He glances at his clipboard and nods in satisfaction. He motions the forklift forward.

The auction space looks a little like a theater. A procession of forklifts is ready to go onto the stage and rows of seats are spread out toward the back. The seats are packed with dozens of people, many with open computers on their laps. You climb up to the third row and slide into the aisle seat.

Turn to the next page.

The auctioneer stands in the center of the stage. Behind him a large screen projects all the auction information—the name of the company, the grade of the beans, and the prices as people bid.

The man with the scar watches from the edge of the stage, a sinister smile on his lips. The fork-lift with the counterfeit Jamoke coffee moves into place. It's really the inferior beans from Kisii—but only you and the man with the scar know that.

The auctioneer calls out, "Lot 249—forty-five bags—grade AA—Jamoke brand. What will you give me to start? Do I hear $360? Yes, $360! Do I hear $370? $370? Yes, to the man on my left, $370!"

You know the beans are counterfeit. You're outraged, but what can you do? The auction is moving along so fast.

Suddenly you stand up and let out a bloodcurdling scream. Everyone stops, frozen in shock, silently staring at you.

Go on to the next page.

Pointing at the forklift in the center of the stage you yell, "Those beans are counterfeit!" You start explaining as quickly as you can about the cover-up you've just witnessed.

With surprising agility the man with the scar climbs the steps and lunges toward you. He's got a knife!

At the last possible second a coffee trader in the second row grabs his hand and wrestles the man with the scar to the ground—but not before the knife has nicked the skin directly above your left eye. A steady stream of blood begins to drip down your face.

Chaos ensues, but once the police arrive, things calm down. The man with the scar is arrested and hauled away to the police station. The chief inspector tells you he wants to question you as soon as a local doctor finishes stitching closed your wound.

You're shaking a bit from shock, but you think it was all worth it. The Jamoke brand has been saved and your family's honor—and fortune—will soon be returned. You smile to yourself, knowing that you'll always wear this particular scar with pride.

The End

You'd love to go after Mjanja, but you worry he's got too big a lead. And frankly the man with the scar terrifies you. You race out of the warehouse and toward the city center.

You stop at a main intersection and look left and right. To your right is a prosperous business street crowded with lots of shops and people. To your left you spot the Java Business Hotel. You know *java* is a slang word for "coffee." This must be a sign! You race toward the hotel and enter the elegant lobby.

It takes a moment for your eyes to adjust from the bright sunlight outside to the cool, darkened interior of the hotel. Then you spot him—Mosi, sitting at a table near the bar, talking with two men.

You run toward him. As soon as Mosi sees the look of terror on your face, he jumps up, nearly overturning the table. You quickly explain what you've seen, but he doesn't wait for you to finish. Within seconds the two of you are racing back toward the Coffee Exchange.

Turn to the next page.

You spot the man with the scar and point him out. Mosi doesn't recognize him but alerts the auction foreman of possible trouble.

The head of auction security captures a photo of the man with the scar from security footage and posts it on Interpol's website. Within minutes there is a reply.

The man with the scar is wanted in connection with a coffee sabotage syndicate operating between Kenya and Brazil. The report states that the police have been tracking him for nearly a year.

The email continues, "The agent in charge of the operation was tragically gunned down. The man with the scar is our chief suspect. You are warned— PROCEED WITH EXTREME CAUTION!"

The head of auction security makes an urgent phone call to the local police. Within minutes several squad cars pull into the auction parking lot. Their lights are off and their sirens are silent. They hope to capture the man with the scar by surprise.

Quietly but quickly auction security, assisted by the Nairobi police, surrounds the man with the scar from every direction. He turns to run but there's nowhere for him to go. The police wrestle him to the ground and firmly fasten handcuffs around his wrists.

You're a national hero! Soon your face appears on the cover of every national newspaper in Kenya. You're given a medal from the KCTA, the Kenyan Coffee Traders Association, and their promise of free coffee for life!

The End

Although you're tempted to trace the coffee sabotage, the next auction is still a few days away. The damage to the crops is happening now. You offer Uncle Bennett and Mosi your assistance. Together you come up with a plan.

You and Mosi ride over with your uncle in his jeep to inspect the damaged area. Just as Mosi had said, nearly a dozen plants have been trampled into the ground. It's a sad sight to see all the crushed branches with their beautiful white flowers still attached.

Glancing around the ground you notice something odd. You call out, "Look at this," sweeping your arm over the area. The two of them walk toward you.

"These look like animal tracks," you say, pointing straight down. "But these," you continue, pointing to your right, "look like footprints from several different-sized boots."

Mosi puts his foot into the smallest footprint. "They must all be large men," he says with certainty. "I wear a size twelve shoe. The smallest print here is much bigger than my foot."

Turn to the next page.

Together you inspect the area more closely. A distinct pattern emerges—sets of hoof prints, possibly from a black rhino, followed by several pairs of human footprints.

"This is not good," Mosi says with a frown. "I think we need to stake out the area tonight." You readily offer to help.

Mosi points to a large log at the edge of the trees near the field. "That should offer us a good viewing spot and a bit of protection, too," he tells you.

At dusk you and Mosi hike out to your hiding place. Although a jeep ride would have been faster your uncle worries that if your vehicle was spotted, whoever is leaving those footprints might run away.

You and Mosi sit in friendly silence as the sky changes from blue to gray to a deep purple. You marvel at how peaceful the landscape seems as the sun sets. It's so tranquil and different from a sunset back home in New York City.

Suddenly your solitude is interrupted by a series of small grunts and the sound of dry twigs snapping. In the dimming light you see a baby rhino walk into the coffee fields. Mosi whispers to you, "He looks about two years old."

Turn to page 34.

You hear heavier twigs snapping nearby. Seconds later you see three large figures, all dressed in black, follow the baby rhino into the field.

Before you can move you hear a hissing sound nearby. It sounds like air leaking from a tire. You turn just in time to see a large snake spring out of a hole in the log and strike Mosi's leg. Its long fangs tear through Mosi's cotton pants and penetrate the skin of his calf.

Mosi lets out a small howl of pain. The snake slithers away.

Clutching his calf Mosi assures you he is fine. You're not so sure. His face is furrowed in pain.

"Go, follow the men," he whispers urgently. "Find out what they're up to before we lose sight of them!"

If you don't follow the men tracking the rhino, it may be too late. Still, it's clear that Mosi is in terrible pain. What if the snake that bit him is poisonous?

If you choose to follow the baby rhino and the mysterious men, go on to the next page.

If you choose to go get help for Mosi immediately, turn to page 40.

You trust Mosi. He knows African snakes much better than you do. If he thinks the snake wasn't poisonous, he's probably right.

Mosi gives you his flare gun and motions for you to go. "If you need help, fire a flare into the sky," he whispers, grimacing in pain. "I told some of my crew to keep an eye out tonight. If they see a flare, they'll come running."

You silently track the men through the fields. You see the baby rhino quickly moving ahead of them. Even though it's a baby, it still weighs more than 2000 pounds. No wonder it tramples everything in its way.

The men stay close to the baby rhino but safely out of its sight. Rhinos are known to have terrible eyesight but a very good sense of smell. With the men behind it and a gentle wind blowing toward them the baby rhino can't sense the impending danger.

Turn to the next page.

Finally the rhino stops and lets out a howl of sorrow. It almost sounds human, it's so distressed. You hear one of the men yell, "There's the mother!" They run forward.

Another man calls out, "Keep the baby back until we finish sawing off the mother's horns. Then just shoot it."

In the moonlight you can see the baby rhino standing next to a large carcass—its dead mother. The men dressed in black are poachers!

They expertly saw off the mother's horn and slowly surround the baby rhino. One of them carries a large semiautomatic rifle. You know it's too dangerous for you to get any closer.

You pull Mosi's flare gun out of your pocket, aim for the sky, and shoot. Its brilliant red tracer illuminates the night sky. Help is on the way!

Turn to page 38.

The men seem frozen in shock. No one moves. Then the man with the gun yells, "We have to get out of here before we get caught!" They run deeper into the coffee fields.

Mosi's crew arrives within minutes. Several run into the coffee fields to look for the poachers. Another directs two men to take Mosi back to the big house as fast as they can. He radios ahead for a doctor.

You and one of the crew stand together side by side, waiting for the Wildlife Protection Officers to arrive. The baby rhino doesn't move but remains next to its mother. He explains to you that baby rhinos stay with their mothers for the first two and a half to three years of their lives. This one is too young to live by itself in the wild.

Go on to the next page.

"Won't another female adopt it as one of her own?" you ask, remembering something you'd seen once on a wildlife TV show.

"No," he says sadly. "Female rhinos raise their own babies. Chances are good the herd would reject this one and it would eventually starve to death."

"But what will happen to it now?" you ask with concern.

He gently replies, "My guess is that it will be sent to the Nairobi Zoo. Maybe later, when it's old enough, they'll try to repatriate it into the wild."

The baby rhino looks stoic by its mother's side. It stands there in silence until the Wildlife Protection Officers arrive.

The End

40

You trust Mosi a lot—but not this time. You saw the snake that bit him and it looked deadly.

You run back to the plantation as fast as your legs will carry you. Uncle Bennett and two other crew members race back in your uncle's jeep to the spot where you left Mosi.

Mosi is unconscious! His leg is very swollen and he's barely breathing.

Together you gently lift him into the jeep. Uncle Bennett drives like a madman, racing back to the house. One of the crew members radios ahead to make sure the local doctor is there when you arrive.

Dr. Portwood quickly examines Mosi's swollen leg. He cuts a small X into the skin on Mosi's calf near the snakebite. Using a battery-operated suction vacuum, the doctor draws out some blood and whatever venom remains at the site. Mosi remains unconscious.

"I need you to go back to the log and capture the snake that did this," he says to you with grave concern. "I'll start an anti-serum drip, but I'm just guessing as to type and dosage. Until we discover exactly what type of snake did this we won't know if Mosi will…"

You don't wait for the doctor to finish his sentence. You and one of the crew members leap into the jeep and race back to your hiding place.

Go on to the next page.

You show the crew member the hole in the log where the snake emerged. He covers the hole with a sisal sack while you pound on the log with a tire iron.

Within seconds you see the large snake slither into the sack, filling it to the brim. He bravely ties a cord around the top and throws the sack into the back of the jeep. Together you hurry back to the house.

The snake is quickly identified as a puff adder, one of the most dangerous snakes in all of Africa. Dr. Portwood adjusts Mosi's anti-venom serum to the strongest possible dose.

Dr. Portwood smiles at you kindly. "He's not out of danger yet," he says, "but your quick action may have saved Mosi's life."

Together you all gather around his bed and wait.

The End

You travel in a convoy of three jeeps to Lake Nakuru National Park, 80 miles northeast of Nairobi. The open-air vehicles carry all your safari equipment and tents, your parents, you, Lee Jong, and a crew of five, including two Masai warriors. One will act as your assistant guide, and the other will manage your safari camp.

You arrive at Lake Nakuru and are over-whelmed by its beauty. *Nakuru* means "dusty place" in the Masai language of Maa. Right now there's nothing dusty about it. The savannahs sur-rounding the lake are a vibrant green, the result of early spring rains. The lake itself seems to move in vibrant pink waves.

"What's that?" you ask in amazement.

You've never seen anything like it. It's as if you were watching the ocean surf, but instead of a blue color, this ocean is pale pink.

Wambua, the older of the two Masai warriors, laughs in delight. "That, my friend, is more than 100,000 flamingos standing together in shallow water." He goes on to explain that the lake is very alkaline and filled with a type of algae and plank-ton that the native flamingos love.

"Some days there are more than a million flamingos on the lake at one time," he tells you with enthusiasm.

Turn to page 44.

44

You look left, then right, then left again. You're amazed by everything you see. You pepper your mother with questions about the park and its animals.

Your mother tells you that Lake Nakuru National Park is now one of the premier rhino sanctuaries in Africa. Rangers have fenced in more than 70 kilometers of land to contain the 100 or so rhinos that live here, including at least twenty-five of the rare black rhinos.

"But why fence them in?" you ask. "Why not let the rhinos just roam free in the wild?"

"The fence keeps the animals safe from poachers," your mother answers. "Rhino horns can sell for more than $25,000 per pound on the black market. Each horn weighs four and a half to six and a half pounds."

"That's crazy!" you exclaim, quickly calculating the numbers in your head. "That means each rhino horn could be worth more than $160,000."

Go on to the next page.

"Sad but true," your mom continues. "It's prized in the Middle East, where it's carved into dagger handles. In parts of Asia it's ground into a powder and swallowed."

She explains that some Asian people mistakenly think it cures fevers and increases strength when ingested.

"Many people say it really works," Lee Jong comments, a gleam in his eye.

Your mother stares at him, frowning in disappointment. Wambua sees your mother's reaction and changes the subject.

Turn to the next page.

You try to get a better sense of Lee Jong by asking him lots of questions. You learn that he's lived in Kenya for eight years and that his father owns an import/export company in Beijing.

Lee Jong studied zoology in China with a specialty in the order *perissodactyla*. He tells you he's thrilled to be on a safari with an expert like your mom.

He seems friendly enough, but there's something about him you just don't trust.

Wambua, on the other hand, is great. He always has a smile on his face and is really friendly. He wears the traditional Masai dress—a deep red-checkered shuka, a colorful piece of cloth, draped over his body. On his feet are cowhide sandals and in his hand is his ever-present orinka, a wooden club the Masai use as a weapon. Secretly you hope he'll never have to use it on this trip.

As dusk settles over camp, you hear a jeep approaching from the distance. Behind the wheel is a woman, about your mother's age, with curly, golden hair. In the wind it looks like a lion's mane.

As she gets closer, your mother stands up and calls out excitedly, "Lara!"

Turn to page 48.

Soon you and your father are introduced to her. "I'd like you to meet Lara Johansson," your mother says with a wide smile on her face. "Lara runs the Kenyan Wildlife Organization. We're old classmates from college."

Lara smiles at you warmly. "When I heard your mom was going to be here, I couldn't resist joining your safari for a few days," she tells all of you. "I've always wanted to know more about black rhinos in the wild. Who better to teach me than your mom?"

Your mom looks delighted by the arrival of her friend. They sit down together to talk.

Lara seems friendly enough, but you think there's something strange about her. She seems a bit edgy and keeps looking around the camp, almost as if she's taking mental notes on who's there.

A sudden thought pops into your head. Lara Johansson = LJ. Could this be the criminal Dr. Abellera mentioned to your mom?

That night, over a dinner of beef cooked with rice and beans, Wambua tells you wonderful tales about his tribe and their herd of cattle. He has a son, Gatimu, near your age.

"Gatimu is about to go through his Moran ceremony," he tells you proudly. "That's our traditional rite celebrating the passage from boyhood to junior warrior."

Go on to the next page.

Wambua tells you that a junior warrior is expected to help protect the land, the village, and all their cattle. You ask him more questions about his son and becoming a junior warrior. Wambua is touched by your interest in the Masai culture and his tribe. Suddenly his eyes light up.

"Why don't you accompany me to my village for a few days to witness Gatimu's Moran ceremony?" he asks with delight. "Your mom can start her research here and we'll catch up with them in a few days."

"What an honor!" your father exclaims. "I bet not many Western kids your age have ever really lived with the Masai."

You're very tempted. It would be amazing to spend a few days in a Masai village, eating, sleeping, and hunting with them—not to mention witnessing the Moran ceremony. Still, you're a little reluctant to leave your parents alone with LJ on safari—whoever that turns out to be.

If you choose to stay with your parents on safari, turn to the next page.

If you choose to go with Wambua to his Masai village, turn to page 77.

50

Your curiosity about LJ outweighs your wish to visit Wambua's village—but just barely. Wambua is gracious in accepting your decision.

"Maybe you can return next Spring Break for a real Masai adventure," he says with a grin. Your father assures you that if your grades remain good this is a distinct possibility.

Early the next morning you stroll into the small tent they've set up as your mom's research lab. It's filled with books on Africa, Lake Nakuru, and black rhinos. A long table in the center holds several maps. You pick up one to study.

"That one divides the park into activity sectors," your mom explains, pointing to different colored grids. "We'll be exploring one grid each day, tracking the local black rhino population."

You open up a thick plastic telescoping tube with a lock and key at the top. Inside is a topographical map covered in colored dots. "What's this?" you ask.

Go on to the next page.

"That's the most valuable map of all," she says a little uneasily. "It's the park ranger's GPS map pinpointing recent coordinates for all the black rhinos in the sanctuary. If it fell into the wrong hands, it would be a treasure map for poachers."

Your mom pulls up a small gold key dangling from her intricately beaded Masai necklace. "But I have the only key," she tells you in a whisper, smiling.

You hear a branch snap directly outside the tent. Your mother continues studying the map, but you quickly unzip the tent flap and watch as Lee Jong strolls away toward the lake. Lara is also nearby. *Was one of them eavesdropping?* you wonder to yourself.

Turn to page 53.

That day you explore the area of the map colored blue, northwest of your camp. You ride in the jeep with your parents, Lee Jong, and Lara. Wambua left this morning to celebrate his son's Moran ceremony. He'll be back in a few days.

Over the next several hours you see lots of baboons, warthogs, and too many bird species to count—but no black rhinos.

Lara is driving. She pulls the jeep over to the side of the road. "Now we'll listen for alarm calls," she tells you. " When an animal spots a predator, it calls out an alarm to warn other members of its group."

"But I thought black rhinos didn't have any predators, except humans." You tell her. "After all they're herbivores, right?"

Your mom joins in. "You're right that rhinos are herbivores and don't eat meat," she says. "But they've been known to attack and kill other animals when threatened. Some, including zebra and eland, definitely see them as predators."

You listen for a few more minutes. No alarm calls yet.

Turn to the next page.

54

You glance to the west and are surprised to see fast-moving black clouds approaching. You point them out to Lara, who looks at them in alarm.

"The Masai call them 'flood clouds,'" she says with grave concern. "They can bring a lot of rain in a very short period of time."

She turns around in her seat and looks at your parents. "I think we should head back to camp—now."

Just then you hear a loud alarm call nearby. Your mother turns and gasps in astonishment as a large black rhino emerges from a stand of trees. It stares at you for several moments and then calmly retreats back into the woods.

You know if you plead to return to camp your parents will agree. On the other hand, you may never see a black rhino this close again.

If you choose to return to camp before the storm clouds arrive, go on to the next page.

If you choose to support your mother's desire to track the black rhino, turn to page 62.

It's only day one. You're confident there will be another black rhino sighting again soon.

With Lara at the wheel, your jeep speeds back toward your camp at the edge of Lake Nakuru. The threatening black clouds have gathered speed. Within minutes they're directly overhead.

CRRRAAACCCKKK!!!

An enormous crash of thunder shatters the quiet. It begins to rain heavily. It's as if someone turned on a faucet above your heads. You've never seen rain like this back home. The water is coming down fast and furious and you can barely see in front of you.

Turn to the next page.

"We can head to higher ground," Lara yells above the roar, "Or try a shortcut across the wooden bridge."

She points to your right. A suspension bridge made from logs sways erratically over a bursting stream.

Looking at the ground you realize that the rain is coming down so fast that it can't be absorbed into the soil. Rivulets of water are joining together to form small streams. If the streams begin to merge, you have no doubt there will be a flash flood.

Your jeep is a solid, fast vehicle. You could probably make it across the bridge if you hurried.

The water under the bridge is raging south, still a few feet below the lowest point of the bridge's foundation. You have to decide quickly.

If you choose to head for higher ground, turn to page 58.

If you choose to take the shortcut and cross the bridge, turn to page 60.

58

You grab your mother's GPS device and switch the receiving channel to capture meteorological satellites. You plug in your coordinates. Its LED radar screen shows a long string of fast-moving rain clouds all around you. This rain is not going to stop anytime soon.

A warning flashes along the bottom of the GPS screen: "Turn Around, Don't Drown." You know what this means. A flash flood is expected. You need to head for higher ground.

Lee Jong yells above the pounding rain, "This is a heavy jeep, but I've seen SUVs swept away by less than two feet of water. We have to climb higher—now!"

You all agree. Lara pushes the accelerator to the floor. You race up a slippery dirt road toward a nearby plateau.

Go on to the next page.

The rain continues to fall at an alarming rate. *This must be what it means when they say it's raining buckets,* you think in terror.

Lara's steely determination is obvious. Her white-knuckled hands tightly grip the wet steering wheel. The jeep lurches to the left and then to the right in the slippery mud. Lara quickly adjusts the steering wheel to keep your vehicle on track.

Within minutes you reach a higher plateau and pull off the road. The rain slowly begins to lessen. Soon it becomes easier to see the landscape below.

You can't believe it. The spot on the road where you were just a few minutes ago is now a raging river caused by a flash flood.

Your mother gasps in horror and points to the south. The bridge is gone! In the distance you see some of the bridge's logs bobbing like toothpicks in the churning water.

You shut your eyes in horror, trying to block out the image of you and your family trapped together in the raging river, floating away forever…

The End

60

There's no time to lose! You grasp the jeep's door handle as Lara races toward the bridge.

The jeep tilts to the left as you hit a slippery patch of road. Lara pulls the steering wheel right. For a few seconds she doesn't have control of the vehicle.

You hydroplane blindly across the wet, muddy surface. Quickly she pulls her foot off the accelerator. The wheels grip the road again. You speed forward.

It feels as if the rain has increased in volume. It lashes your face as it falls, stinging your eyes and making it hard to see. You grip your father's arm in terror.

"Hold tight everyone!" Lara screams above the roar. She pushes the accelerator to the floor and the jeep lurches up onto the suspension bridge.

Go on to the next page.

You travel just a few feet onto the bridge before a wave of brown water washes over the top of the jeep. You're thrown overboard by its force.

You try to scream, but as you open your mouth it fills with muddy water. You feel yourself caught in a whirlpool, spinning around and around.

Suddenly you know it's true. Images of your life flash before your eyes as the end approaches.

You see your mother and father sitting together in your New York City brownstone, looking terribly sad. You see your teachers and friends, hugging one another with tears in their eyes. You see your bedroom ceiling once more in the morning light—and then everything goes black.

The End

You agree with your mother. This is too good an opportunity to pass up. Lara steers the jeep sharply toward a narrow road that parallels the forest.

She drives slowly. "There!" you whisper quickly, pointing to your left. You see the black rhino's shadow as it moves through the woods.

You know that rhinos have terrible eyesight, but a keen sense of smell and acute hearing to make up for it.

Every few minutes the rhino stops and intently stares back at you. She seems to be gauging your level of threat. So far, so good—she's done nothing to suggest she's about to attack.

The black rhino moves a little farther into the woods, making it difficult to see her. You stop and wait. A few minutes go by but she doesn't emerge from the woods. Still, your mother feels confident that she's nearby. She carefully marks your GPS coordinates on her map.

"Based on the animal's size I think she's a female. I bet she's gone back to her crash," your mother says.

She explains to you that although rhinos are generally solitary animals, mothers and calves sometimes live together in small groups after they've given birth. Such a group is known as a crash.

"That means there may be a lot of rhinos all together in one place," Lee Jong says excitedly. Is it your imagination or does he have a menacing gleam in his eye?

Go on to the next page.

Lara looks up quickly and stares at Lee Jong. Her eyes narrow in focus.

Your mother seems troubled. She suggests you all go back to camp for dinner, and then she'll return later to this exact spot for some night tracking. She invites you along.

Lee Jong looks dejected but hides it well. He knows her invitation doesn't include him.

"I have to make an important satellite call tonight anyway," he says quickly. "I'm fine staying behind at camp."

Lara begins to ask him a question, but your mother cuts her off. "I could also use your skills tonight, Lara," she says. "Why don't you join us?"

Lara hesitates for a moment but then readily agrees to accompany your mom on her night's adventure.

You're tempted to join them, as night tracking sounds exciting. Yet this may be your only chance to watch Lee Jong up close and listen in on his call…

If you choose to track the black rhinos by night, turn to the next page.

If you choose to remain at camp and spy on Lee Jong, turn to page 71.

The idea of spending an evening with your mom and Lara, tracking rhinos and their babies in their native habitat, is just too tempting.

After a delicious dinner of grilled meats and cornmeal cakes you, your mom, and Lara climb into the jeep. Your dad is going to stay behind at camp and catch up on some reading.

With Lara at the wheel you head back out in the jeep. Using your mother's handheld GPS device, you guide Lara back to the spot where you saw the black rhino enter the woods.

"Did you mark the spot on the GPS map back at camp?" you ask your mom.

"I did," she replies, reflexively reaching for the key on the chain around her neck.

Suddenly she looks distressed. "I must have left the key in the lock back at camp," she says with concern. Lara bites her lip.

Go on to the next page.

After a few moments of silence your mother says, "Oh well—your father will probably use my research tent as his reading room tonight. I think the GPS map will be okay."

You're not so sure. The thought of Lee Jong examining the unlocked GPS map is almost enough to make you insist on turning around.

Just then you hear a series of grunts from inside the woods. It's time to track the rhinos. Together you creep into the woods, as quietly as possible. In a clearing ahead four large female rhinos are standing close together. They watch as three smaller rhinos use their lips to strip leaves off a nearby wild plum bush.

Your mother quickly scribbles something in her notebook. Through a series of hand signals she and Lara agree to move closer to the rhinos. You'll all approach from different directions.

Turn to the next page.

You walk to the right, feeling your way in the dark. You step on a thick branch that snaps under your weight. You freeze in fear.

A huge female rhino turns toward you and lets out a loud snort. Her ears are flattened back against her head and she looks angry.

The black female rhino quickly lowers her head and charges toward you. Her enormous horn is aimed straight at your chest!

There's a tree to your left and an open clearing to your right. Should you climb the tree or try to run for it?

If you choose to climb the tree to escape the charging rhino, turn to page 68.

If you choose to run into the clearing, turn to page 69.

68

You leap up and grab the lowest branch of an acacia tree. Years of running track have strengthened your muscles. You can move with great agility.

The acacia tree is full of wickedly sharp thorns. You don't even notice all your bleeding scratches until you're safely several branches above the ground.

The huge rhino grunts and makes a trumpet sound below you, sniffing the air to try to pick up your scent. You shiver in fear but remain very still.

After what seems like a lifetime, the huge rhino turns around and goes back to her group.

Your see your mother point to the west. In the distance you can hear the sound of a jeep quickly approaching. Suddenly you see Lara behind the wheel of the jeep. She's driving at record speed.

All the rhinos look startled and confused. You can't believe Lara was quick enough to reach the jeep without a rhino charging her. You appreciate the skills she's learned living on this land.

Your mother jumps into the jeep while it's still moving. Lara races over, stopping directly beneath your acacia tree.

The rhino that charged before now sees you in the tree. She turns toward you, coming at you once again.

"Jump!" Lara yells. You do as you're told. You land with a painful thump on the floor of the jeep.

Lara races away from the clearing. The rhino continues to chase after you. Thankfully the jeep moves faster than the charging animal.

You've escaped the rhinos today—and promise yourself you'll be more careful when you return to track them tomorrow.

The End

You're a fast runner. Running toward the clearing is your best option. After all, how fast can a 4,500-pound animal really go?

You think you've outrun the rhino. Glancing back you're surprised to see she's gaining ground.

You try to swerve as you run, making her stumble behind you. The rhino seems able to turn on a dime. You had no idea these animals could be so agile. Then you remember something you once read. The black rhino is related to the horse. It's surprisingly nimble. When charging, it can reach speeds of more than thirty-five miles an hour.

Her ears are flattened against her head, a definite sign of anger. You face forward, running as fast as you can.

Turn to the next page.

Without any further warning you suddenly feel the tip of the black rhino's horn slash the back of your leg. You fall to the ground as she lets out a howl of anger above you. She rears back and stabs her horn near your knee. You scream in agony and roll over.

You fall down a small slope. Looking up, you can see the black rhino has no idea where you've gone.

You know rhinos have terrible eyesight. She sniffs the air hungrily, trying to catch your scent.

It takes all your strength and courage not to scream in pain. Slowly the rhino moves away from the edge of the slope.

What seems like a lifetime later, your mother and Lara slide down the hill to rescue you. Your mother looks terribly worried. Lara quickly examines you.

"Nothing's broken," she whispers to your mother. "But you'll need lots of stitches," she says to you. "Let's get out of here before that rhino returns."

The most important thing is that you've escaped with your life. And you promise yourself—this will be the last time you ever underestimate the amazing speed of a charging rhino.

The End

You wave goodbye as the jeep carrying your mother, father, and Lara heads off into the darkness. You told your mother you were really tired and planned to go straight to bed.

Just before they left, you saw Lara and Sabra, the Masai warrior who manages your safari camp, having an animated conversation by the kitchen tent. Lara looked really worried. After talking for a few minutes, Sabra hurried down a goat path toward the south while Lara returned to the jeep.

What's that all about? you wonder to yourself.

While the rest of the crew cleans up after dinner, you make a big point of yawning loudly and repeatedly, making sure Lee Jong sees you. He's busy fiddling with his satellite phone.

Turn to the next page.

Without a mobile transmitting tower anywhere nearby, his regular cell phone won't work. His satellite phone is an Iridium 2000 zx. You're enough of a tech geek to know that's a very expensive phone.

Lee Jong repeatedly looks at his watch. He sees you eyeing him and casually explains, "I'm calling a different time zone. I need to keep an eye on the clock to catch them as they wake up."

How big a time zone difference? you wonder to yourself.

You sit by the campfire and pretend to nod off, abruptly waking yourself as your head touches your chest.

"I'm whipped," you say, yawning once again. "Too much excitement for one day." You wish him a good night and walk toward your tent.

A few minutes later you turn off your battery-operated lantern and wait in the dark. You see Lee Jong watch your tent intently before slowly walking toward the lake. Soon you can see a flashlight moving near the desk in your mother's research tent. You catch the gleam of the golden key as it opens the tube with her GPS map. The flashlight briefly illuminates the face of Lee Jong as he unrolls the map and begins taking notes. A few minutes later he stuffs the map back into the tube, locks the latch, and leaves the tent.

Just as you suspected—Lee Jong is stealing your mother's research! But why?

Go on to the next page.

You creep out of your tent and lie down in the tall grass near the campfire. This should be a perfect vantage point to listen in on Lee Jong's phone call.

Soon you catch a glimpse of him near the campfire. He picks up his Iridium 2000 zx and starts dialing a bunch of numbers. After a moment's hesitation you can hear someone answer on the other end.

"Ni hao," they say loudly in Chinese. "Hello, hello?"

"It's me," Lee Jong says quickly. "I found her GPS map. I've got all the coordinates. How fast can Ku and his gang get here?"

He listens intently to the person on the other end. A sinister smile creases his face.

"Perfect," he says excitedly. "We should be able to get three, maybe four, really good horns. At $160,000 per horn we'll be rich!"

You gasp in horror. He's talking about poaching your mother's beloved black rhinos!

Turn to the next page.

Just as you're about to leap up and yell for help you hear a motor rapidly approaching.

A huge open-air truck roars to a stop near the campfire. Seven Kenyan Wildlife Rangers, armed with semiautomatic rifles, jump from the vehicle. The tallest one yells, "Lee Jong—you're under arrest!"

You look up and see Sabra sitting in the seat next to the driver. He must have alerted the authorities to possible trouble.

I bet that's what Lara was discussing with him before she left, you whisper to yourself under your breath.

Lee Jong runs into the tall grass near you. Instinctively, you throw out your hand, catching him by the ankle as he trips forward. Two Wildlife Rangers hold down his squirming body as they tightly clamp handcuffs around his wrists.

The tall ranger approaches you and thanks you for your fast thinking.

"We've been watching Lee Jong for several months now," he says gravely. "Ever since there was a surge in black rhino poaching in our national parks."

He continues, "Through KWO we traced one of the rhino horns to Lee Jong's father's company in Nairobi. We've been waiting for him to strike again."

Turn to page 76.

You helpfully show the ranger Lee Jong's satellite phone and explain what you've overheard. Your mother, father, and Lara arrive as you're telling your tale.

"I thought you promised me you were going right to bed," your mother scolds you loudly, worry in her voice. "If I even suspected you'd be involved in this whole thing...I, I could never forgive myself if something happened to you..."

The head ranger cuts her off. "We were nearby the whole time," he assures your mom. "There was never any real danger—but the kid did help to break up an international poaching ring."

When your mom's not looking, the head ranger winks at you.

Your information is vital to breaking up an international poaching ring operating in Asia and the Middle East. Your mother immediately puts the Wildlife Rangers in touch with the FBI. They've also begun tracing the illegal rhino horns in the United States.

Your mom looks exhausted yet relieved. Now she can focus on her real passion—searching for majestic black rhinos in Africa.

The End

You and Wambua walk along a narrow path for two hours. You're far away from your camp at Lake Nakuru but very close to his village.

Soon, below you in a clearing, you see a dozen straw and mud huts and a large cattle pen. A thick fence of thorny branches surrounds the village.

Wambua proudly explains, "A traditional Masai village is made up of many inkajijik, small huts made of branches woven together. A plaster of mud, grass, and ash is smoothed over the branches to make them waterproof."

You admire the sound structure of the huts. "The men in your village are good builders," you say with approval.

Wambua laughs. "You mean the women, my friend. When a girl gets married, her mother, sisters, and the other women in the village help her build her new enkaj, her new home. It's where the family will sleep, cook, eat, socialize, and store all their possessions. It's her castle, as you say."

Turn to the next page.

"The men are responsible for the enkang, the thick acacia fence surrounding the village," Wambua continues. "At night we bring all our cows, goats, and sheep inside the fence so they're not attacked by wild animals."

You're greeted as an honored visitor to the village. A cool mug of fermented goat's milk is given to you to drink. You sip it slowly, admiring the beautiful Masai women with their beaded necklaces and heavily pierced ears. The men are all tall and thin. Everyone looks amazingly strong and healthy.

Turn to page 80.

Wambua's son, Gatimu, is very friendly. He proudly shows you around the village and introduces you to everyone you encounter. You meet all his friends and cousins, including Aza, a girl cousin whom he introduces to you as his best friend.

Aza is a year younger than you but just as tall. Her hair is very short. Around her long neck she wears a dozen strings of beads. Her eyes twinkle when she smiles and you can tell she's a little mischievous.

Soon you, Gatimu, and Aza are good friends, planning many adventures during your short stay together.

Gatimu tells you all about his Moran ceremony, which is in two days. There will be a lot of music, dancing, and special food. At the end of the ceremony he must prove his bravery by finding a lion and holding its tail.

"I have a happy surprise for you," he says with a sparkle in his eye. "I've asked my father if you can join me and he's said yes!"

"What an honor," Aza says to you excitedly. "I'm also a bit jealous. Girls aren't allowed to play with lions."

You smile and try to look brave. Holding a lion's tail? Suddenly your life back in New York City seems very tame in comparison.

Go on to the next page.

You spend the next morning with Gatimu exploring the area around the village. In the afternoon Aza comes to find you.

"Good news!" she says excitedly. "We've found a sleeping black rhino. We're going to play our favorite game. Come on!"

You run with Gatimu and Aza to a nearby watering hole. Gatimu tells you along the way about a traditional Masai game called "The Rock & the Rhino."

"We take turns approaching a sleeping rhino, placing small rocks on his back. The last person to place a rock before the rhino wakes up is the winner," he says merrily.

Before you can reach the watering hole Wambua hurries up the path. "There you are," he says excitedly. "I have a big surprise for you and Gatimu. Follow me!"

He starts to quickly walk back toward the village. You're not sure what to do. You love surprises. On the other hand what are the chances you'll get to play "The Rock & the Rhino" again during your visit?

If you choose to follow Wambua for a surprise, turn to the next page.

If you choose to play "The Rock & The Rhino," turn to page 108.

You love surprises. You hope there will be another chance to play "The Rock & The Rhino," but for now you and Gatimu say a quick goodbye to Aza and happily follow Wambua back toward the village.

"How about giving us a hint or two?" you plead with Wambua.

He laughs out loud. "What's the point of a surprise if I give it way? You'll see soon enough. Follow me."

You take a short cut down a narrow goat path to the edge of the enkang fence surrounding the village. Wambua stops, pivots toward you, and smiles. You and Gatimu look around. You don't see anything unusual or "surprising."

"Well?" Wambua asks, grinning expectantly. You look around again. Nothing stands out. Suddenly you hear faint whistling from above. You know that song! It's "Java Jive." Glancing up you see you father smiling down at you from the thick branch of an Acacia tree.

"Dad!" you yell.

Go on to the next page.

Your father leaps from his branch and lands at your feet. He gives you a big bear hug. Wambua and Gatimu stand next to you, grinning from ear to ear. You should be embarrassed, but you're just so happy to see you dad. You can't wait to tell him about all your adventures with the Masai.

A quick look of concern crosses your face. "Where's Mom?" you ask quickly. "Is she okay?"

Your dad assures you everything is fine. "She's spending the day near a watering hole," he says. "She wants to film black rhinos interacting with other animals. As soon as I heard one of the Masai crew was coming here to stock up on honey,…"

Gatimu quickly interrupts him and turns to Wambua. "Is it true? Are the Aweer coming today with honey?"

Turn to the next page.

"Surprise number two," Wambua says happily. "The Aweer are on their way with plenty of honey for our Moran celebrations."

Wambua and Gatimu fill you in. The Aweer are a tribe that specializes in harvesting honey. "They don't farm or raise cattle like we do," Wambua tells you. "For generations they've supplied many of our tribes with the delicious honey we use for cooking on special occasions."

"The amazing thing," Gatimu says excitedly, "is that they train songbirds to find the beehives."

Gatimu explains that the Aweer search for natural hives by teaching their songbirds a special tune. The birds fly around, surveying the landscape. When they spot a hive, they sing back the Aweer's song.

Turn to page 86.

Gatimu continues, "Then tribal members climb a tree, smoke out the bees and take some—but not all—of the honey."

"They leave some of the honeycomb behind," Wambua explains, "so the bees can rebuild the hive. Later the Aweer can come back to take more honey from the same hive. They're very smart."

A few minutes later some of the Masai children come running into the village followed by a dozen members of the Aweer tribe. They're tall like the Masai but have rounder bodies. They wear animal-skin sarongs and glass-beaded necklaces. They have wide smiles and look very friendly.

The older members carry large drum-shaped containers that hold the honey. The younger ones carry woven-reed cages with several birds inside. One carries a stick with four empty beehives attached to it.

A senior tribe member senses your curiosity and tells you, "These birds are known as the best talkers and can easily learn our songs."

You, Gatimu, and the other Masai children begin to ask lots and lots of questions. The Aweer are very patient and happily answer your queries.

Soon you learn that honeybees have been producing their sweet nectar for millions of years. The type of flower the bees visit determines the taste and color of their honey. The Aweer have brought the best kind to the Masai, golden Acacia honey.

Turn to the next page.

You also learn that honeybees have a nectar pouch inside their bodies. They fly from flower to flower, gathering the nectar and pollinating plants along the way.

"The bees carry the nectar back to the hive and seal it inside honeycomb cells," one Aweer man tells you. "Each bee colony has their own distinct odor so they can smell their way home."

"What about the birds?" Gatimu asks excitedly. "How do you teach them to spot hives and sing?"

The Aweer laugh. "Those are some of our special secrets," the most senior tribesman says. "But if you like, I can show you a little with some of our new birds," he continues, pointing to the cages.

"These birds are great mimics," he says. "It takes a lot of patience to teach them our more complicated songs but for today we'll concentrate on simple six- or seven-note tunes."

He opens one of the cages and gently cups a gray parrot in his hand. "We'll sing a song to the bird, show her a beehive, and repeat the song again," he continues. "Once she sings it back to us, we'll give her a cashew nut as a reward."

He puts the bird directly in front of his mouth. In his other hand, he holds one of the empty beehives. He whistles a short tune to the bird, holds up the beehive, and whistles the tune again. He repeats the process over and over and over again.

Go on to the next page.

The bird watches his mouth intently. Soon she begins to anticipate the end of the song and glances at the beehive. After what seems like the fortieth or fiftieth time the tribesman whistles the tune, the bird finally sings the song after the beehive is placed before her.

Many of the Masai laugh and applaud. A tribesman suggests releasing the bird to see if she can find any local beehives.

"I have an even better idea," Wambua says with a gleam in his eye. "How about a competition? We'll pair off and whoever finds the most honey wins."

The senor tribesman agrees. He suggests each competing pair choose a bird and the Aweer will help train them.

The pairs start to form. Some children pair off with their mother, father, or siblings.

"So what will it be?" Wambua says to you and Gatimu cheerfully. "Fathers versus sons or father-and-son teams?"

Gatimu grins at you. On the one hand, it would be great for the two of you to team up. He knows the landscape well, and you bet together you'd locate a big hive in no time at all. On the other, it would be a lot of fun to pair off with your dad to see how well you could do together.

If you choose to pair up with Gatimu, turn to the next page.

If you choose to join your dad in a search for honey, turn to page 102.

90

You and Gatimu join hands and raise your arms in the air like victors.

"Kids versus adults!" Gatimu yells.

A tall, lean, Aweer tribesman smiles, picks up a birdcage and a beehive, and motions you over toward a far corner of the village. Together you sit on the ground. He opens the birdcage, gently cups the parrot in his hand, and pulls her out.

"First you need to decide on a song," he tells you.

You and Gatimu discuss your options. You don't seem to know any of the same tunes. Gatimu knows many African songs and you know none. You know lots of American songs, but he doesn't recognize any of them.

Then Gatimu suggests the "Elephant Song" and hums a few notes. It sounds an amazing amount like the beginning of "Happy Birthday."

"Perfect," you tell him.

The tribesman hands Gatimu the bird, tells him to put her in front of his mouth and whistle the first six or seven notes of the song. You sit next to him and together you whistle in unison.

At first the bird looks perplexed, tilting her head to the side and staring at you intently. Over and over you whistle the tune, show the bird the beehive, and whistle it again. Just when you think you can't whistle anymore because your lips are starting to go numb, the bird sits up, shakes her head, and whistles the tune back to you.

Turn to page 92.

Gatimu is so excited he almost releases the bird into the air. "Not just yet," the tribesman says, laughing. "She deserves a treat."

He hands you a cashew nut. "Try again," he instructs you, "Just to make sure she knows your song. If she sings it back, she's ready."

You do as he suggests. The bird repeats the song immediately, eyeing the cashew the whole time. When she's finished, she quickly cracks the nuts and eats the pieces.

The tribesman tells you to carry the bird to a spot where you think there may be honey, sing the song to her, and release her into the air.

"Once the bird finds a hive, she'll fly back to the village on her own," he tells you as he gives you a handful of cashews to take along as the parrot's reward.

Go on to the next page.

The tribesman also gives you a small smoke can to slow down the bees inside the hive, and some matches to light the cotton cloth that will produce the smoke. He explains that the smoke makes the bees docile, allowing you time to cut away some of the honeycomb without getting stung.

You gently place the parrot in your shirt pocket, thank the tribesman for his help, and head off in search of honey.

Gatimu directs you toward a watering hole a few kilometers away. He says there are many large Acacia trees nearby. He thinks it's your best bet to find a large beehive, a lot of honey—and victory!

Twice before your reach the watering hole you stop near small groves of trees, take the parrot from your pocket, whistle your tune, and release the bird into the air. Both times she swoops gracefully over and under the treetops. Both times she returns to you without repeating the song.

Turn to the next page.

As you approach the watering hole, you can see a group of large Acacia trees shading the area. Together you and Gatimu walk among the trees, glancing upwards, looking through the branches for a beehive.

Near the top of the tallest Acacia tree you spot what looks like several sheets of honeycomb hanging close together. You point it out to Gatimu.

"That's strange," he says looking up into the tree. "The Aweer didn't say anything about honeycombs outside of a beehive."

"But look at the size of that thing," you say excitedly. "There's got to be several pounds of honey just sitting there, waiting for us to grab it."

Gatimu isn't convinced. He suggests using your parrot for confirmation. You hold the bird near your mouth, whistle your tune, and toss her upwards. She promptly glides toward the honeycomb and hovers nearby, her wings flapping wildly.

Go on to the next page.

Much to your surprise she quickly turns and flies off into the distance, back toward the village. Neither you nor Gatimu heard her sing your song.

"Something's wrong," Gatimu say warily. You brush off his concerns and offer to climb the tree for a closer look. You secure the smoke can to your belt, put the matches in your pocket, and start to climb.

As you get nearer the honeycomb, you hear an increasingly loud drone from the bees inside the hive. When you're two branches below the hive, you excitedly yell down to Gatimu, "There are at least five sheets of honeycomb! Even more than we expected. I'm going to light the smoke can and climb up..."

YEOW! Before you can continue a bee stings you on your finger. Suddenly there are three bees on your arms, then five, then nine. Looking up you can see more bees are coming your way.

Turn to the next page.

"It's a swarm!" Gatimu yells from below. "We have to get out of here!"

You rapidly leap down, branch to branch, until you're on the ground. There's now a full swarm in progress. There must be over a thousand bees buzzing around you.

"Run!" Gatimu screams to you. He starts to sprint back toward camp.

"No," you yell. "It's too late. We'll never outrun the swarm. Quick—jump into the watering hole!"

If you choose to follow Gatimu and run back toward camp, turn to page 98.

If you choose to leap into the watering hole to escape the swarming bees, turn to page 100.

You run as fast as your feet can carry you, scurrying after Gatimu to keep up. You see him briefly stumble, swatting several bees from his neck as he yells in pain.

Three bees zoom in and buzz by your ear. Another bee lands on your cheek. All four of them sting you at the same time.

"ARRGGHHH!" you yell in agony. You're too afraid to stop. You can hear the loud drone of the bees right behind you. You run faster and faster, gasping for breathe.

You're nearly back at camp before you notice that Gatimu has slowed his pace. Quickly he goes from running to fast walking to a dead stop.

You race up next to him, sweat pouring off your face.

"Shhhhh," he says. "Listen."

You stop and listen. At first the only sound you can hear is your heart pounding inside your chest. When it slows you realize you hear nothing but sweet, golden silence. You've outrun the swarm!

Together you stumble into camp and begin to tell your tale. Gatimu's mother applies a poultice of something dark and gooey on all of your bee stings. It brings immediate relief.

"You boys are lucky," the Aweer tribal leader tells you with a grave face. "Those weren't honeybees. Those were African killer bees."

Go on to the next page.

You gasp in horror. "They don't build traditional hives but just sheets of honeycomb attached to braches," he continues. "Not only are they very aggressive but they produce hardly any honey. They're too busy out looking for trouble and cannibalizing good honeybee hives."

Gatimu explains where you found the hive and two tribesman set out to find and destroy the killer bee hive. The Aweer respect all living things but not when they threaten their livelihood.

"Deaths from killer bees are very rare," the tribal leader continues, "Especially if you're not allergic to their sting. Still, you boys were lucky."

"And next time, trust your bird," he says gently. "I bet she didn't sing for you—but she raced back here at record speed."

You and Gatimu nod in agreement. You've never felt so lucky in your lives!

The End

100

There are bees in your hair, on your arms and in your ears. They're all over you! You don't have enough time to outrun them.

Without another thought you run toward the watering hole, take a deep breath, and leap into the cool, dark water. The shock of the water shakes the bees from your skin. You swim deeper, eager to get as far away from the swarm as possible.

You glance up and see a huge splash as Gatimu leaps into the water near you. He glances around, a look of terror on his face. He sees you and swims deeper.

Through hand signals he tells you to follow him toward the shore. You can't hold your breath much longer. It feels like your lungs are about to explode.

Together you swim to shallower water and look up. Are those clouds moving above you in the sky or is the swarm hovering over the water's surface?

Gatimu signals again, telling you to slowly surface and catch a breath. The murky water clears a bit as you reach the top. You lips break the water's surface and you take a deep breath.

A small bee climbs into you mouth and stings you on the lip. You suppress a scream and head back down. The swarm is right above the water! There's nowhere to escape.

For a moment you lose sight of Gatimu and try not to panic. Then he swims toward you holding out two reeds he's cut from the rushes near the shore. They're stiff and hollow. He mimes putting one end in your mouth and the other above the water. You can use them like straws to breath.

Go on to the next page.

Together you sit on a slippery rock about three feet below the water's surface. Gatimu takes one end of your reed and crushes it in his fingers. He pushes it above the surface and breathes in and out, hungry for oxygen. You do the same.

The bees continue to hover above the water but they can't touch you. You realize that by crushing the reed's end Gatimu has frayed its edge, making it impossible for bees to climb inside. Gatimu is brilliant!

Time passes slowly. Your skin feels waterlogged but you could care less. You'll happily sit here until you're sure the swarm of bees is gone and you can walk home safely.

Together you sit in the dark, murky water and wait.

The End

You and your dad smile at each other. There's no doubt you'll make a great team.

"Victory is ours!" your father whispers to you, quoting a line from your favorite movie.

The tallest Aweer tribesman hands you a cage with a small African Gray Parrot inside. He gives your father the smoke can, the cotton fuel, and some matches. You follow him to a log beneath an Acacia tree where he starts your lesson.

He shows your dad how to light the cotton. Once ignited, it will produce lot of cool smoke. The tribesman shows your dad how to pump the handle back and forth to make the smoke come out the top of the smoke can. After you spot a beehive, you're supposed to send smoke inside, wait ten minutes and then do it again. After the second smoking, the bees will be tame enough for you to harvest some of the honeycomb without getting stung.

"Next, you must choose a song to teach your bird," the tribesman tells you. You look at your father and immediately know you are both thinking the exact same thing.

"Java Jive," you say in unison, laughing.

The tribesman hands you the parrot and has you hold it in front of your mouth. You whistle the first seven notes of the song, hold up the beehive like the tribesman showed you, and whistle the tune again.

Go on to the next page.

You do this over and over again for what feels like a very long time. No luck. The parrot looks interested, but she hasn't sung your song back to you yet.

You father suggests the two of you whistle the song together. You sit side by side and begin. The bird looks even more intrigued, glancing from you to your father and back to you again.

Success! Soon she whistles the tune back to you. You whistle it once more, and she repeats it again. This is almost too much fun. The tribesman seems amazed by your quick success. He gives the parrot a cashew nut, which she promptly devours, and gives you an extra handful as you begin your quest.

Turn to the next page.

As you're more familiar with the area, you lead your father toward the high, grassy plains where you saw a group of tall, wide trees when you were out playing with Gatimu. Soon you come upon a large group of tall, green trees with branches heavy with brown fruit.

"Gatimu said these are called 'sausage trees,'" you tell your dad. "Can you guess why?"

He laughs as he picks up one of the enormous brown fruits that have fallen from the tree. Looking up you can see dozens more still attached to their branches. "Because these huge things look like sausages?" he asks.

Turn to the next page.

"Exactly," you answer. "Gatimu said they can weigh over ten pounds each. He said the Masai have a saying—"If you sit beneath this tree too long you won't last forever. If the falling fruit doesn't kill you then the elephants will get you when they come to eat the fruit."

The parrot in your pocket begins to stir. "I think she senses something," you tell your dad hopefully.

Gently you hold the bird in your hand and whistle the beginning of your song to her. She flies straight into the air, above the tallest sausage tree and circles the grove. Back and forth she flies, above and below the canopy of trees. Suddenly your hear her sing the first notes of "Java Jive."

"Honey!" your dad says excitedly. You and he follow the parrot's call and find her on the branch of a sausage tree in the middle of the grove. Something that looks like a beehive sits perched above her in the dark recesses of the tree.

Your dad lights the cotton fuel and pumps the handle back and forth. As soon as some smoke comes out of the top, he starts climbing the tree. You watch from below, the parrot is now perched on your shoulder enjoying her cashew treat.

"It's a good-size hive," you dad whispers loudly. He pumps smoke into the hive and climbs down a few branches to wait. After ten minutes he climbs up and pumps some more.

"Just two minutes more," you say, barely able to conceal your excitement.

Go on to the next page.

You dad climbs onto the branch next to the hive. He gently taps it to see if any bees are stirring. He gives you the thumbs up and gently reaches into the hive.

You can barely watch. You worry that he'll get stung or won't find any honey. After what feels like a lifetime, a big smile creases his face and he pulls out a large, dripping piece of honeycomb. He puts it into the canvas bag on his shoulder, reaches in, and pulls out another. Then he climbs down to you to show you the haul.

The honey is a deep caramel color and smells very sugary. "I left enough for a future harvest, just like the Aweer said," your dad says proudly.

You both pop a piece of honeycomb into your mouths and start walking back toward the village. It tastes amazing—sweet and rich and syrupy.

"I don't even care if we win," you say to your dad. "This was such a fun adventure!"

Your father agrees. "We make a pretty good team," he says proudly. Together you whistle "Java Jive" the whole way back to the village.

The End

108

The game sounds dangerous but too much fun to miss. You, Gatimu, and Aza reach the watering hole and spot an enormous sleeping rhino a dozen yards away.

Gatimu goes first. He picks up a small brown rock, about the size of an egg, and creeps toward the sleeping rhino. He quickly puts it on his back and then races away.

Aza goes next. She walks very slowly toward the rhino. When she is next to it, she leans down, picks up a good-sized rock, gently places it on the rhino's back, and backs away. All the children make low whistling sounds. Aza has shown great courage.

Gatimu points to you. You're up next.

Turn to page 110.

You pick up a small black rock and quietly approach the rhino. You're shaking with fear but try to appear brave.

Seconds after you place the rock on his back, the black rhino's eyes roll open and he quickly stands up. The other children scream and scurry away.

You run to a tall acacia tree and scramble up the trunk, just out of reach of the huffing, puffing, stomping rhino below.

The sharp thorns on the acacia tree leave scratches up and down your arms. They hurt but given the alternative, they're nothing like the wounds a charging rhino could cause.

You climb onto a high branch and wait. You don't care how long you have to stay here you're not coming down until the rhino is long gone.

Just above your head you hear a quiet hissing sound. Your turn and see a long green snake hanging from a thin branch. His tongue darts in and out of his mouth as he watches you.

"Green Mamba," Aza yells below you. "More dangerous than a rhino! Don't move or he'll bite."

If you leap from the tree, you'll land directly in front of the black rhino below.

The snake moves a little lower, its head swinging back and forth. He stares directly into your eyes.

If you choose to leap from the tree, turn to page 112.

If you choose to stay where you are, turn to page 124.

You have an irrational fear of snakes. You leap from the tree but nearly land on top of the enraged rhino.

The rhino opens his mouth and lets out a horrible growl. It sounds like a trumpet being crushed by a steamroller. You crouch on the ground and make a leap toward some tall grasses to your right.

The grasses help camouflage you. You remain very still. You can hear the angry rhino sniffing and snorting near you. He seems to be getting closer.

Just when you're certain he's discovered your hiding place you hear Aza yell at the rhino while Gatimu throws something at him. A pointed stick lands near your head. The rhino is briefly distracted and turns away. You get up and start running.

The rhino briefly chases Gatimu, but he's very clever, running and hiding behind the trunk of a giant fig tree. He can't be seen.

Go on to the next page.

A sudden breeze from behind makes the rhino stop, turn around and madly sniff the air. He's lost Gatimu's scent. Soon the rhino hurries off to the left, chasing an unsuspecting zebra that has stumbled onto the scene. The rhino is fast but the zebra is faster.

You're exhilarated and shaking with adrenaline. Gatimu congratulates you on winning the game and asks if you're okay.

"I'm fine," you assure him with a smile. "But next time I'm going to pass when it comes to playing "The Rock & The Rhino."

"Agreed," says Aza, her eyes sparkling in mischief. "Next time we'll stick to something simple— like ostrich races."

That evening Aza invites you to join her and her mother as they make a special soup for the Moran ceremonies. All the women in the village are making something special to eat during the celebration. Aza and her mother, Dodo, have chosen to make Groundnut Soup.

Turn to the next page.

114

Aza's younger sisters have spent the afternoon gathering the peanuts they planted near the cow pen last year. As you'll be feeding the entire village, they've gathered hundreds and hundreds of the nuts. You, Aza, her sister, and mother spend over an hour shelling the peanuts before you'll roast them.

Wambua and Gatimu tease you when they spot you shelling the nuts with Dodo and her daughters.

"In the Masai tribe the women are responsible for the cooking and the men for raising the herd," Wambua tells you with a quick smile.

"Not in my tribe," you counter, with a laugh. "Both the women and men cook. In fact, some of the greatest chefs in New York are men."

This makes Wambua and Gatimu laugh out loud. They think you are joking.

Turn to page 116.

116

After you finish roasting the peanuts, you help spread them out on a cloth laid on the ground so they can cool. Once they're no longer hot to the touch, you, Aza, and her mother take turns grinding them up. The peanuts go into a large wooden bowl, and a large wooden pestle is brought down on them, again and again, until the nuts are ground into a paste.

It's very hard work and soon you are sweating. After all the peanuts have been ground, Dodo puts them back into the roasting kettle. She and Aza add a lot of water and throw in some spices. The mixture cooks for a while until it is thick.

It smells amazing, and you can't wait to try it. Until then you'll have to be satisfied with the peanut smell clinging to your hands. After handling all those peanuts, you smell like the inside of a peanut butter jar!

You're exhausted from all your hard work helping to make the Groundnut Soup. You and Gatimu lay on grass mats in his family's inkajijik. It's a little crowded inside with his mother, father, and baby brother nearby. Still, there's something wonderfully cozy about the entire family being so close together.

You drift off to sleep in the middle of Gatimu telling you a story about the soft fur of a baby cow. In your dream you imagine petting the cow and feeling its velvety coat.

"That's funny," you think to yourself. "I can feel its fur crawling up my arm."

Go on to the next page.

Suddenly your eyes fly open. You tense up. Something velvety is definitely crawling up your arm—and its not related to the cow family.

Looking down you see an enormous spider creeping up your arm, one hairy leg at a time. He's not moving fast, but you're paralyzed with fear.

"Gatimu!" you hiss loudly. The spider stops in place. Gatimu stirs in his sleep nearby.

"Gatimu!" you say a little louder with panic in your voice.

"Don't move!" Wambua answers urgently. "That's a King Baboon Spider on your arm. It's very aggressive when disturbed."

Turn to the next page.

Gatimu is now sitting up, alarmed. "He must have been attracted to the peanut smell on your hands," he whispers quickly. "Tarantulas love ground peanuts."

"Tarantula!" you whisper in panic. "I thought you said King…"

Wambua answers before you can finish your sentence. "The King Baboon is in the tarantula family. He'll probably crawl off you in a minute. Just try not to move."

The hairy red spider takes a few more steps up your arm. He's now near your shoulder. If you move quickly, you can probably fling him away.

If you choose to stay calm and hope the spider will crawl away, go on to the next page.

If you choose to throw the spider off you— now!—turn to page 121.

"Stay calm. Stay calm," Wambua says to you, over and over, in a soothing voice.

The spider continues to slowly crawl up your arm. He reaches your shoulder and begins to move toward your neck.

"He's just exploring," Gatimu says, trying to sound relaxed. You can hear the fear in his voice.

The King Baboon Spider creeps across your collarbone and stops when he reaches your neck. Looking down you can see his eight hairy red legs and large round body.

You squeeze your eyes shut. You don't think you can stand another minute of this. You're holding your breath, terrified the spider will crawl up onto your face if it senses movement.

Turn to the next page.

With incredible agility Wambua scoops up the spider with his bare hand and tosses him into a clay bowl. He moves so quickly the spider doesn't have a chance to sink his fangs into Wambua—or you.

Wambua places a cloth over the bowl and motions for you and Gatimu to follow him outside. Together you walk in the moonlit darkness to the edge of the enkang, the thick acacia fence surrounding the village.

It's amazingly calm outside. You breathe in deeply, enjoying the cool night air.

Wambua lowers the bowl to the ground, tips it on its side, and pulls the cloth away. The King Baboon Spider hesitates for a moment, then quickly crawls out and scurries beyond the fence.

"These spiders eat crickets and mice," he tells you, watching the spider hurry away. "Both of them bother our cattle so we see the King Baboons as our little friends."

You smile to yourself. There wasn't anything "little" about the spider crawling up your body. And you doubt you'll ever refer to him as your "friend."

The End

You can't stand it another second. The King Baboon continues to slowly creep up your body. It reaches your shoulder in few seconds.

The spider pauses for a second and then begins to crawl toward your head. You can feel every one of his eight legs in motion. It takes all your concentration not to scream.

Wambua continues to gently remind you, "Stay calm. Stay calm."

Easy for him to say, you think. I'm the one with the little hairy beast crawling toward my face.

You swiftly sit up and move your hand toward your neck, hoping to flick the spider away. The spider begins to slide down your chest, his legs moving wildly as if trying to grasp the air.

When your hand reaches the spider, he leaps out and deeply sinks his fangs into your thumb.

"AARRRGGGHHH!" you scream in pain.

Turn to the next page.

122

You instinctively swing your hand away from your body. The King Baboon spider flies off your hand and hits the wall. He drops to the ground, stunned. In a few moments he recovers and moves at record speed toward the door, as frightened of you as you are of him.

Wambua grabs your hand and swiftly examines the bite. He looks up at Gatimu and says urgently, "Quick! Get me my knife."

Wambua has you elevate your arm. He asks Gatimu to tightly grasp your wrist to slow the blood flow from your hand. He then makes a small incision into your thumb directly below the spider bite. You try not to scream again from pain.

Wambua lowers his lips over the incision. Creating a vacuum he begins to suction the spider venom out of your bite and into his mouth. He turns and spits the liquid out onto the floor. He repeats this action two more times, making sure as much of the spider's venom as possible has been removed.

Go on to the next page.

Gatimu's mother quickly mashes up a poultice of herbs and ash. She gently applies it to your wound, and then tightly wraps your hand in a linen bandage.

You can feel the spot where the spider's fangs penetrated your skin. It hurts like a very bad hornet sting—only ten times worse. The area around the bite feels warm and tender.

Gatimu tells you he plans on sitting up the rest of the night, watching you.

Wambua explains, "I think I got out most of the venom but maybe not all."

He continues cautiously. "If you have an allergic reaction to the King Baboon's venom, your heart will begin to race and you may start to hallucinate."

Gatimu sees the panic on your face and tries to reassure you. "I think you'll be fine but we'll know soon."

You lean against the wall, exhausted and sore. You can't help wondering what would have happened if you stayed calm. Would the spider have wandered away on its own? You'll never know.

You and Gatimu sit together in the darkness and wait.

The End

You remain as motionless as possible. The green mamba drops a few inches lower and peers directly into your face.

He's only an inch or two away now. You force yourself not to blink and hold your breath.

The green mamba flicks its tongue near your ear. You hear a light "tkk" as its head brushes your hair. It takes all your concentration not to scream.

Slowly the green mamba swings back and drops down onto your branch.

Within seconds you realize he no longer has any interest in you. He slowly slithers away. Stretched out like that you realize he's over nine feet long.

You watch as the green mamba climbs the trunk and disappears into the branches above.

Go on to the next page.

You gasp for breath. It's safe on the ground again as the rhino has moved away. The Masai children gather around you, slapping you on the back and cheering your bravery.

Gatimu put his hand on your shoulder and happily tells you, "You've had a double lucky day—first escaping from a black rhino and then from a green mamba."

You just hope your good luck holds out for the rest of your visit.

Turn to the next page.

126

Back in the village you help with preparations for the Moran ceremonies. The villagers dress in vibrant colors, and both the men and women wear lots of intricately beaded necklaces, earrings, and belts. They give you a blue and red shuka, some cowhide sandals, and a multicolored necklace to wear.

Aza wears four sets of blue and red beaded earrings in each ear. She looks stunning. For one crazy second you think about getting your ears pierced, so you can wear more of the beautiful Masai jewelry. Then you think about having to tell your parents and let the idea pass.

The boys being initiated as young warriors get white zigzags painted on their faces. This gives them a frightening warrior look.

The ceremony is led by the village's laibon, the highest figure in the Masai religion. There is much singing and dancing, including the famous Masai jumping dance.

A circle is formed around the young warriors. One or two take turns in the center. They stand upright and near each other, jumping as high as possible without letting their heels touch the ground. They jump higher and higher, until exhausted, while members of the tribe yell encouragement. You think Gatimu jumps the highest of all.

Turn to page 128.

128

After the dance there is a big feast. You eat an amazing array of dishes you've never tried before including roasted goat and mutton, fermented milk mixed with animal blood, and honey mixed with fat.

At the end of the celebration, Aza wishes you well as you and Gatimu prepare to head off on your quest to hold a lion's tail. Wambua pats the tops of both of your heads seven times for good luck. Aza does the same.

You leave the village accompanied by two elder warriors who will protect you and verify your successful quest.

You walk for miles before you spot a pride of lions in the distance. There are six females and ten cubs circled close together. Two big males stand off to the side.

You wait a long time, hoping one of the males will separate from the group or fall asleep. You and Gatimu agree there's no reason to antagonize two lions at once…

Finally the larger lion moves away from the pride and toward a nearby stream. You and Gatimu quietly discuss which lion you should approach.

The one near the pride is smaller but might feel more protective of the group. The one near the stream is larger but looks less agitated.

If you choose to approach the lion near the pride, turn to page 130.

If you choose to follow the lion to the watering hole, turn to page 132.

Together you and Gatimu walk, hand and hand, as slowly as possible toward the lion near the pride. You feel a little shaky. You can feel Gatimu's sweaty hand in yours.

The lion watches you approach, silently. He seems both curious and calm. Even though he's the smaller of the two male lions you bet he weighs at least 500 pounds.

You avoid direct eye contact. This could make the lion see you as a threat. You're close enough now to hear his rhythmic breathing.

Go on to the next page.

Gatimu walks one step ahead, guiding you toward the lion's back. Very quickly yet quietly he gently grasps the lion's tale and holds it up.

The lion turns his enormous head and intently stares at Gatimu. The lion's breathing accelerates.

Before Gatimu releases his hold, you quickly touch the thick fur at the tip of the lion's tail. Together you beam at one another and begin to slowly walk backwards toward the elder warriors.

Out of nowhere a large female appears, rushing toward you. She stops a few feet away, throws her head back, and releases a loud growl. You and Gatimu freeze in place and grip each other's hand more tightly.

The eldest warrior throws his sharp spear. It lands near the lioness' feet. He's purposefully missed her body but is demonstrating his strength. She glares at him and then very slowly walks back toward the pride.

You've successfully held a lion's tail—and lived to tell about it!

The End

132

You and Gatimu follow the larger lion to the watering hole. The enormous animal gracefully lowers his head to the water and drinks. He doesn't seem to notice you.

Hand in hand you and Gatimu approach the lion from behind. Slowly and gently Gatimu reaches for the lion's tail. With amazing agility the lion turns, rears back on his haunches, and let's loose a ferocious growl. Its so loud it makes your teeth shake.

The older warriors distract the lion using the calls of a herd of eland. Eland are large, deer-like animals and a favorite meal for lions.

The lion hesitates, glares at you but begins to move away. He must be hungry. The promise of fresh eland is too much for him to pass up.

"Eland are much more delicious than a couple of skinny kids," Gatimu whispers to you gratefully under his breath.

Your quest to hold a lion's tail has failed, but the elder warriors assure you they'll tell of your bravery back at the village. You begin your trek home.

Halfway back to the Masai village, the eldest warrior stops and points to the sky. A strange black cloud is moving toward you. It changes shape over and over as it gets closer.

"A swarm of tsetse flies," Gatimu yells in fear.

He quickly turns to you. "Do what we do. Now!"

Go on to the next page.

The Masai crouch on the ground, trying to make themselves as small as possible. They cover themselves with their bright shukus. You do the same.

Within seconds you can hear the flapping of thousands of tiny wings as the tsetse flies swarm near you. The loud buzzing lasts for a few minutes. Then everything is silent.

Certain the swarm has moved on, you peak out from under your shuka. Gatimu looks at you and smiles. His smile quickly turns to a frown. A large winged tsetse fly is sitting on his exposed foot.

He raises his hand to smack it, but it swiftly flies away. In the spot where the tsetse fly rested there is now a large red welt. Gatimu has been bitten!

You mother warned you that tsetse fly bites could cause a horrible disease known as African sleeping sickness. If Gatimu doesn't get medicine soon, he may die.

The elder warriors don't think they can run back to the village in time. You offer to race there instead.

They worry you won't remember the way. You've never had a great sense of direction—but this is a matter of life and death!

If you choose to run back to the village for help, turn to the next page.

If you chose to stay behind with Gatimu, turn to page 136.

134

You're fast on your feet. You leap up and start running.

You may have a bad sense of direction, but a combination of fear, adrenaline, and luck guides you. You make a few wrong turns but reach the village within a few hours.

Panting and nearly out of breath you tell Wambua what has happened. Aza stands nearby, a look of terror on her face.

Together with the village's laibon, or shaman healer, Wambua quickly brews a tea made from various barks, dried roots, and water. He pours the medicine into a calfskin bladder and ties it onto his beaded belt.

You get ready to leave. Aza reaches out and touches Wambua's shoulder.

"Uncles, please," she says with tears in her eyes. "Gatimu is like my brother. I must go with you to help him."

Wambua quickly nods. Together the three of you set off on foot, racing against time.

Go on to the next page.

You're able to describe the location accurately. Aza knows exactly where it is. With amazing skills she takes short cuts down narrow goat paths. You reach Gatimu in record time.

The elder warriors have laid Gatimu between them and are using large fig leaves to fan his sweating body. Gatimu has a high fever and aches in his joints.

Wambua gently holds the calfskin bladder to his son's lips and coaxes him to sip it slowly. You can tell from Gatimu's expression the liquid tastes horrible. Still, he knows it will make him better.

Aza tells you that, thanks to your quick running, they have reached Gatimu in time.

Wambua nods in agreement. "Gatimu may have a fever for a day or two but he's out of danger," he says to you thankfully. "To me—and my village—your bravery shows that are now a Moran warrior, too."

The End

136

You know that you can run fast, but your bad sense of direction worries you too much. What if you got lost or didn't reach the village in time?

The elder warriors depart on foot, leaving behind two spears, some water, and a little dried beef for you and Gatimu. You hope they return soon.

Gatimu is quiet. As time passes, you can tell he has a fever.

"My legs ache," he moans over and over, his body covered in sweat. You worry that soon he will become delirious.

Go on to the next page.

The sky changes from white to blue to a dusky purple. Darkness is approaching. You hear animal calls in the distance.

Once night descends, you'll be in total darkness. You leave Gatimu for a short time to gather some wood.

You pile a few logs and twigs together, stuff some dried grass in between and start a fire. It burns brightly for a few hours but then begins to fade away.

You grimace in agony. You didn't gather enough wood to keep the fire going through the night.

As the fire burns down, your level of fright increases. Gatimu thrashes about, in the throes of a high fever. He's too sick to move. You can't leave his side to gather more wood.

You try to make the fire last as long as possible, knowing it's your only protection against nighttime predators. You hear the snapping of branches in the nearby woods. You pray it's the elder warriors returning with help.

Scanning beyond the fire you see a pair of eyes, then two, in the tall grasses. You recognize the female lions from the pride.

The fierce one who growled at you looks from you to Gatimu and back. She licks his lips. You swallow hard and wait.

The End

About the Illustrators

Gabhor Utomo was born in Indonesia. He moved to California to pursue his passion in art. He received his degree from Academy of Art University in San Francisco in spring 2003. Since his graduation he has worked as a freelance illustrator and has illustrated a number of children's books. Gabhor lives with his wife Dina and his twin girls in the San Francisco Bay Area.

Vladimir Semionov was born in August 1964 in the Republic of Moldavia, of the former USSR. He is a graduate of the Fine Arts Collegium in Kishinev, Moldavia, as well as the Fine Arts Academy of Romania, where he majored in graphics and painting, respectively. He has had exhibitions all over the world, in places like Japan and Switzerland, and is currently Art Director of the SEM&BL Animacompany animation studio in Bucharest.

About the Author

Alison Gilligan grew up in New England before moving to New York City for college, work, and life (not necessarily in that order). After graduating from NYU she worked in an art auction house and advertising agency before relocating to the Pacific Northwest. There she helped combat international piracy for a large software company before leaving to focus on raising a family and serving on nonprofit boards dedicated to promoting literacy and combating homelessness. She currently lives with her family in Florence, Italy, where she worships at the shrines of Brunelleschi, Bronzino, and mozzarella di bufala. She continues her volunteer work with a nonprofit dedicated to restoring Florence's art treasures. Ms. Gilligan and her family spend their summers on San Juan Island, Washington.

For games, activities, and other fun stuff, or to write to Alison, visit us online at CYOA.com